DATE DUE

Read-About® Geography

Mexico

By David F. Marx

Consultant
Linda Cornwell, Coordinator of School Quality
and Professional Improvement
Indiana State Teachers Association

Children's Press®
A Division of Grolier Publishing
New York   London   Hong Kong   Sydney
Danbury, Connecticut

Visit Children's Press® on the Internet at:
http://publishing.grolier.com

Designer: Herman Adler Design Group

Library of Congress Cataloging-in-Publication Data

Marx, David F.
  Mexico / by David F. Marx.
    p. cm. — (Rookie read-about geography)
  Includes index.
  Summary: An introduction to Mexico, its geographical features, people, and business.
    ISBN 0-516-22041-1 (lib. bdg.)   0-516-27086-9 (pbk.)
    1. Mexico—Juvenile literature. [1. Mexico.] I. Title. II. Series.
F1208.5.M38   2000
972 21—dc21   99-043654

Welcome to Mexico. This is a beautiful land of beaches, volcanoes, and deserts. Rain forests, towns, and huge cities are also found here.

People who live in Mexico are called "Mexicans." Most speak the Spanish language.

Mexico City is the country's capital and largest city.

UNITED STATES

Rio Grande

Gulf of California

MEXICO

Central Desert

Mexico City ✪

▲ Orizaba Mountain

PACIFIC OCEAN

Gulf of Mexico

MEXICO

Caribbean Sea

BELIZE

GUATEMALA

EL SALVADOR

MEXICO

SCALE   1 inch = 400 Miles

0   400 Miles

0   640 Kilometers

North

West ✦ East

South

Mexico lies south of the United States. To the south of Mexico are the countries Guatemala, Belize, and El Salvador.

Much of Mexico looks out on water. To the west is the Pacific Ocean. To the east are the Gulf of Mexico and the Caribbean Sea.

Caribbean Sea

Orizaba Mountain

Almost everywhere in Mexico, you can see mountains rising into the sky. The highest mountain is Orizaba. Its peak (top) is 18,700 feet (5,700 meters) high.

In some places, the dry air and heat creates deserts.

This is the Central Desert, where the ground is covered with rocks and sand.

14

In other places, a lot of rain helps to create areas called tropics.

In the tropics, jungles are thick with trees, vines, and flowers. Hot air and lots of rain makes them grow.

Farmers in Mexico's tropics grow foods like coffee, bananas, and coconuts.

Maize (corn)

Tortillas

Farms in other parts of Mexico grow rice, beans, maize (corn), and many other crops.

Maize is used in many Mexican foods, such as tortillas.

Farming is a common way
to make a living in Mexico.
But people hold many
other kinds of jobs, too.

Some are miners. They dig
into the ground for oil,
iron, silver, lead, or salt.

Miners

Shoe factory

Restaurant

In cities, people work in offices, stores, and factories.

A lot of other Mexicans work for hotels, airlines, and restaurants. They help the millions of people who visit Mexico every year on vacation.

Mexican artists are known for their colorful crafts.

Mexican crafts

Weavings

Women and girls make
weavings like these.

Folk dancing is popular
at Mexican festivals
and during holidays.

Visitors to Mexico love
to explore the jungles,
swim off its beaches, and
shop in the cities and towns.

Maybe you'll visit Mexico
someday, too!

29

Words You Know

Caribbean Sea

Central Desert

crafts

folk dancing

30

Mexican

Mexico City

Orizaba Mountain

tortillas

tropics

weavings

Index

About the Author

David F. Marx is an author and editor of children's books. He resides in Connecticut.

Photo Credits

©: Liaison Agency, Inc.: 14, 31 bottom left (Robert Burke); Peter Arnold Inc.: 25, 31 bottom right (Jesús Carlos); Robert Fried Photography: 17, 22; The Image Works: 29 (Bachmann), 5, 31 top right (Macduff Everton), 4, 31 top left (Michael Wickes), 18 bottom, 31 center right (Alison Wright); Tony Stone Images: 3 (Cosmo Condina), 13, 30 top right (Robert Frerck), 24, 30 bottom left (Bruce Herman), 26, 30 bottom right (David Hiser), 9, 30 top left (James P. Rowan); Woodfin Camp & Associates: 10, 18 top, 31 center left (Robert Frerck), cover (Suzi Moore), 21 (Kal Muller).

Map by Bob Italiano.